When Rudy Crowed

By Martha Tolles

Illustrated by Jon Davis

🪶 Dominie Press, Inc.

Publisher: Raymond Yuen
Project Editor: John S. F. Graham
Editor: Bob Rowland
Designer: Greg DiGenti
Illustrator: Jon Davis

Published by:

ṗ Dominie Press, Inc.

1949 Kellogg Avenue
Carlsbad, California 92008 USA

www.dominie.com

1-800-232-4570

Paperback ISBN 0-7685-2067-3
Printed in Singapore by PH Productions Pte Ltd
1 2 3 4 5 6 PH 05 04 03

Table of Contents

Chapter One
Something Must Be Done

*C*ock-a-doodle-doo!

When Mindy heard her new pet rooster crow in the mornings, she stirred in her bed and smiled.

"Hi Rudy!" she called out. She loved her beautiful brownish-red rooster, and

she loved to hear him crow in the morning. Her dad had given Rudy to her as a birthday present. Rudy was a real farm rooster. Mindy's dad had given some legal help to a farmer out in the countryside. The farmer couldn't afford to give him money for his work, so her dad accepted Rudy as payment, instead.

Mindy could see Rudy from her bedroom window. His house was a chicken coop that Mindy and her dad built together. There was a window in front covered with a wire screen where Rudy could see the world, and where he could tell when it was morning.

It was such fun for Mindy to get up in the morning and go outside to Rudy's coop. She fed him cracked corn, filled his water dish, and patted his soft feathers. Mindy thought Rudy was the best pet anyone could have. Her dad agreed.

"Maybe one day we can get a chicken, too," her dad said.

But not everyone loved Rudy. The neighbors felt differently. Even though their houses were spaced far apart, with fields between them, the neighbors slammed their windows shut when Rudy crowed his noisy crow.

Mr. Gump leaped up from his bed and shouted, "Darn that bird. He wakes me up every morning."

When Rudy crowed, all the dogs in their yards barked happily back at him, making more noise than ever.

"It can't be time to get up yet," grumbled Griselda and Gary, the young parents of twins who lived across the street.

And Miss Fizzy, two houses away,

already seated at her piano, scolded,
"All that racket. How can anybody hear
the notes? I need to practice before my
pupils arrive. Something must be done."

Finally the neighbors came to see
Mindy and her parents. "You must get rid
of that noisy rooster," they said. "We
can't stand it any longer."

"We're so sorry," her parents said.
"Don't you think you might get used to
the noise?"

"Wouldn't you like to see him?"
Mindy offered.

But the neighbors said no, thanks
anyway, and they didn't think they
would ever get used to the crowing.
Mindy was in despair. What could she do?

Chapter Two
No, Rudy, Don't Sleep

Mindy's friend Anna came over to see Rudy the next afternoon. Mindy led Anna down to Rudy's fenced-in yard.

"Oh, he's cool," Anna said. "You've got to keep him."

They watched the reddish-brown

rooster as he pecked hard at the ground, chasing a bug.

"And he helps, too," Mindy said. "He eats all those bugs and keeps them out of my mom's vegetable garden."

"That's great," Anna said. "My aunt has a pet parrot, but all he does is talk. He's really noisy."

"Well, I wish I could teach Rudy to be quieter," Mindy said. Rudy just cocked his red-combed head and looked at her with sharp eyes.

Mindy kept thinking about it after Anna left. How could she keep Rudy quiet? Suddenly, she had an idea. She could keep Rudy up late this evening so he'd wake up later in the morning.

First she placed a small radio near Rudy's coop, with music playing. But he didn't pay much attention to it. Then, during the evening, she kept bringing out little snacks for him to eat. She also closed the door to his coop so he couldn't go inside and roost on the long beam and go to sleep.

Rudy stood at the door to his coop for most of the evening, looking tired. He wanted to go inside so he could sleep, but Mindy wouldn't let him.

"You can't go to sleep just yet," Mindy told him.

Later, at bedtime, she knew Rudy would have to be let into his coop for the night. Then she had an idea. She took her flashlight with her when she and her dad went down to the coop. They found Rudy perched on top of a basket in his yard. His feathers were all fluffed out so he could stay warm, and his eyes were closed.

"No, Rudy, don't sleep," Mindy begged.

13

"I don't see how you're going to keep him awake," her dad said. He picked up Rudy and carried him into the dark coop.

"I'll just leave my flashlight in here, turned on, so it's nice and bright," Mindy told her dad. "I don't like to sleep with the light on in my room. Maybe Rudy feels the same way."

Chapter Three
Over the Limit

*C*ock-a-doodle-doo!

There was Rudy's usual early-morning crow. Mindy glanced at her clock and groaned with disappointment. And in the neighboring houses, Mr. Gump slammed his window, Miss Fizzy missed the right notes on her piano, and Griselda tiredly rose out of bed to to take care of her crying twins.

That evening the neighbors came to see Mindy and her family again. "That bird is too loud," Mr. Gump said.

"We've called a noise consultant," Miss Fizzy added. "He's coming this afternoon."

Luckily, the noise consultant arrived just as Mindy was getting off the school bus. He was a big man, and he carried a piece of equipment.

"This sound meter will measure the decibel level so I can see how loud your chicken is," he explained to Mindy and her mother.

"Rooster," Mindy corrected.

The man cleared his throat. "Now, where is that bird?"

While her mom led him out to Rudy's fenced yard, Mindy quickly ran into the house to get treats for Rudy, some soft fruit and salad from last night's dinner. Maybe she could keep Rudy quiet. Then she hurried outside and put the food in Rudy's food trough. Rudy followed her into the coop and hungrily began to peck at the treats. Mindy felt hopeful.

The man clicked a button on his sound meter and followed Rudy into the coop.

"Come on, fella, let's hear you." The man clapped his hands.

Rudy only looked up at him.

"So, you're going to be that way," the man said. Mindy watched in amazement as the man threw back his head and shouted, "Cock-a-doodle-doo!"

Rudy stopped pecking at the food.

He lifted his beak, flapped his wings and crowed a loud, fine "Cock-a-doodle-doo!"

"Hey, that wasn't fair," Mindy protested. "You tricked him into it."

"It doesn't matter," the man said. "A chicken sounds the same, day or night."

"Rooster!" Mindy said, scowling.

The man peered down at his sound meter. "Definitely over the limit. That sound is not legal. I'll have to report it at the next city council meeting."

Mindy was in despair. "Oh, Mom, let's go to that meeting. And I can take Rudy so they'll see how terrific he is."

Chapter Four
Just Too Noisy

At the council meeting, Mindy set Rudy down next to her.

"Now, be quiet," she whispered to the rooster. "When they see you they'll let me keep you, I bet."

But part way through the meeting

there was some loud clapping. And Rudy
stood straight up, lifted his beak, and
crowed, *Cock-a-doodle-doo!*

The audience laughed. Someone
shouted, "Turn him into Sunday dinner."

The council members frowned. The
mayor said, "I'm sorry, but that rooster is

just too noisy. You can't annoy your neighbors any longer. You'll have to do something about it."

Mindy felt desperate. There must be some way to save Rudy. As they drove home, she thought about Anna and her aunt's parrot.

"I need to call Anna," she told her parents.

Anna's phone was busy, so Mindy sent her an e-mail: "What does your aunt do when her parrot makes a lot of noise?"

In a little while, there was an e-mail from Anna: "I asked my aunt. She keeps him quiet at night by throwing a cover over his cage. But how could you do that with Rudy?"

"Dad, Mom," Mindy said. "I think we need a lot of black cloth."

Chapter Five

More than One Way

Mindy and her dad hurried out toward Rudy's coop. Mom had searched around in her sewing materials and found a big piece of cloth, dark enough to keep out the sun, but light-weight enough to let in some air.

Rudy was in the coop, perched up high on his long beam. He didn't make even a peep while Mindy and her dad tacked up the cloth over the window.

"Now," Mindy said, skipping for joy, "Rudy won't know it's morning until we take it down, will he, Dad?"

Dad chuckled. "Maybe we can fool him. We'll see."

Mindy was so excited, she could hardly go to sleep that night.

When Mindy woke up in the morning, everything was very quiet. There were no sounds from Rudy. She glanced at her clock. It was seven-thirty already. She jumped from her bed and rushed out to the kitchen.

"It worked!" she shouted to her mom. "I finally figured out a way to keep Rudy quiet."

"Good." Mom smiled. "There's more than one way to solve a problem, isn't there?"

"Oh, yes, yes," Mindy said. "And Anna helped me."

"Hey, I helped, too!" Dad said. "And I can still help."

He and Mindy put up some snaps and fasteners to the outside of Rudy's window and to the black cloth. That way, it would be easier to put up and take down the cloth.

Each day after that, Rudy was quiet until Mindy went outside and took down the cloth. When Rudy crowed, *Cock-a-doodle-doo!* it was so late in the morning that people were already awake. No one slammed their windows shut, and no one came over to complain that the noise was too loud.

Mindy was thrilled with her success. She hoped that the neighbors were happy now, and that she could still keep Rudy.

Then one evening the neighbors came to Mindy's house. "I missed a big business deal because I overslept," Mr. Gump complained.

"And I'm not finding time for my practice in the mornings," Miss Fizzy said.

"And I can't get up in time to feed the twins," Griselda said.

"Let that rooster crow," they chorused.

So after that, Mindy let Rudy wake up early, and every morning Rudy happily crowed, *Cock-a-doodle-doo!*